D0121646

DRINKING GAMES

Published by Crazy Coyote Games, PO Box 12, Diss, IT22 1YA.

ISBN 978-0-9557304-0-5

Printed in China

AN ADULT DRINKING GAME
COMPENDIUM

Contained in this book are the rules to 50 all-time great drinking games. They can be played either at home or in the pub — all you need is a sense of fun and a full glass.

FORFEITS

It is in the nature of drinking games that a forfeit has to be paid by any player who fails to perform the task in hand satisfactorily. Inevitably the forfeit is to take another drink, which makes the player's task that little bit more difficult on the next round. We strongly recommend that a non-alcoholic beverage is consumed as a forfeit. It is up to the players to agree the forfeits beforehand and to ensure they are met. Drinking forfeits are measured as fingers of drink so that you line your fingers up against the liquid in your glass and drink to the bottom of one, two or three fingers.

MASTER OF CEREMONIES

It is most important that a Master of Ceremonies be appointed either for the whole evening or a different MC before each game. It is imperative that the MC does not drink any alcohol in order to fully carry out his or her responsibilities. They must monitor alcohol intake of all players and they must ensure that no-one drinking alcohol operates a vehicle. The MC's duties are wide-ranging: they must adjudicate on any disputes, make sure that the rules are abided by and that everyone gets a taxi home or a ride with someone sober.

The other players MUST address the MC as 'Sir' or 'Madam' throughout the game and must always request permission to speak to them. Any other form of address or indeed any show of disrespect, renders the offending player liable to pay a forfeit.

The Master of Ceremonies has the right to impose forfeits, at any time, on any player, utterly at his own discretion and without the need for an explanation. In fact, he can be as biased and as prejudiced as he pleases! He should be helped in this task by a 'Chief Sneak'.

This coveted position of Chief Sneak is awarded to the player who 'sneaks' most often on his fellow players. He should report to the Master of Ceremonies any cheating, general bad behavior and, most particularly, any 'undue spillage' of a drink.

Players may also like to implement the practice of having half-hour hands.

For half-hour periods, players are obliged to drink their drink using one particular hand. Thus, they must take all their drinks with their right hand from on the hour to 29 minutes past and their left hand from the half hour to a minute before the hour. Half-hour hands can last for as many hours as the MC orders. Again the Chief Sneak can help in reporting any mistakes.

Please read the warnings at the back of this book before playing any of these drinking games. Failure to do so may result in serious injury or death.

We seriously recommend that you play these games with non-alcoholic beverages.

AVIATORS

CRAZY COYOTE

**ESTABLISHED SO LONG
AGO WE'VE
FORGOTTEN
WHEN**

AVIATORS

This is a game to be played in a house with a large number of rooms, or alternatively, on a pub crawl. Players form a large conga line and the leader is the 'pilot'.

The conga flight travels from room to room (or pub to pub). Each room visited is designated a country and related drink (Guinness for Ireland, Pernod for France), which the 'passengers' must drink.

The conga line then wends its way onto the next destination. The pilot has responsibility for negiotiating any turbulence, crash landings or air sickness amongst the passengers.

GAMES OF DISTINCTION

ONLY THE FINEST INGREDIENTS

BALANCING ACT

Crazy Coyote

ESTABLISHED IN NINETEEN HUNDRED AND EIGHTY-EIGHT

CGG GAMES LONDON

BALANCING ACT

EQUIPMENT: TWO CANS OF DRINK PER PLAYER

Draw a line on the floor to mark the starting point. Players take it in turns to stand behind the line with an unopened can of drink in each hand. They should rest each can on the floor, in front of the line. The idea is to move one can at a time, gradually edging each one further forward holding on to the games at all times.

When a player has reached as far as they can, they must leave one can there. Then all they have to do is stand up again — without touching the floor! Thus they have to work their way back with both hands gripping the one can.

The player who places the can furthest away is the winner. Any player who touches the floor has to pay a drinking penalty.

BLIND
MAN'S BLUFF

FINEST

ONLY   HOPS

QUALITY

PERFECTION IS
OUR PROFESSION
CRAZY COYOTE
OF LONDON

ESTD   1988

BLIND MAN'S BLUFF

EQUIPMENT: TWO BLINDFOLDS

Players split into two teams. At one end of the room is a table with a drink for each team member on it.

The first player in each team is blindfolded, turned around ten times and then has to try and negiotiate their way to the table to down their drink.

Once they have done this, they must return to their team and hand the blindfold to the next player. Team members are allowed to shout out directions.

The winning team is the first to drink all their drinks.

CRAZY COYOTE

BOAT RACE

"only the finest ingredients"

BOAT RACE

Players form two teams. Each team stands in a line facing the other and every team member should have a full drink.

On the word "Go!", the first player must down their drink and put their empty glass on their head. This is the signal for the next team member to start drinking.

The winning team is the one that finishes first and it is customary for the losing team to buy the victors their next drink!

BULLSEYE

EQUIPMENT: A GOLF BALL

This is a variation on 'tag'. Play starts when a player succeeds in dropping a golf ball in someone else's drink without them noticing. That player is now 'it'.

Once they have finished their drink they can retrieve the ball and use it to get their own back — at an opportune moment, of course. Players with a full drink are the most obvious targets!

If a player is spotted dropping the ball in by another player they must drink a four-finger forfeit. If the ball bounces off the table or misses its target completely, then the player has to finish their drink as a penalty.

This game can be played with a coin instead of a golf ball for a subtler version.

This is the famous Bunnies Game. We know of no game produced which cost so much to manufacture. Our traditional skills and dedication make a game unequaled in the history of the world.

GENUINE

GENUINE

Estd

1988

Bunnies®

KING OF GAMES

Produced by traditional methods and only the finest ingredients

Crazy Coyote Inc.

BUNNIES

The starter points their two index fingers at another player, thereby nominating them as the 'bunny'. The 'bunny' must respond immediately, by putting their thumbs to their temples and waggling their bunny ears; at the same time, repeating "Bunny, Bunny, Bunny…". The player on the 'bunny's' left must raise and waggle their right ear only, and the player on the 'bunny's' right must waggle their left ear only. Waggling must continue until another 'bunny' is selected.

The 'bunny' passes the go to someone else by removing their hands from their head and pointing their two index fingers at another player, who (along with those on either side) must start waggling ears appropriately.

'Bunnies' may fake passing the go by pointing at another player with thumbs still firmly pressed to their temple — this is a false pass. BUT, if the person pointed at foolishly starts behaving like a 'bunny', they pay a major drinking forfeit; those on either side, a minor forfeit.

CAPTAIN BLUFF

OBJECTIVE: TO AVOID GETTING INTO A TANGLE!

The nominated player starts by saying "Captain Bluff takes his first drink of the evening". On saying this the player picks up their drink with thumb and ONE finger, takes ONE sip, puts it down tapping it ONCE on the table, taps their right shoulder with ONE finger on their left hand, taps their left shoulder with ONE finger on their right hand, taps their right shoulder with ONE finger on their right hand, and finally taps their left shoulder with ONE finger on their left hand.

Once all players have succeeded in doing this, they move on to Captain Bluff's second drink of the evening, using TWO of everything, and then his third drink using THREE of everything, and so on.

ANY mistake at all results in that player having to pay a drinking forfeit, and then trying again!

Cereal Madness®

EL
JUEGO
MAS
FINO

ESTD 1988

CRAZY COYOTE
LONDON

CEREAL MADNESS

EQUIPMENT: AN EMPTY CEREAL BOX, SCISSORS

The box is placed on the floor and players take it in turns to pick up the box using only their mouths. No part of your body must touch the floor, except of course your feet!

Each player is given three attempts. If they touch the floor, fall over or have to stand up again, their turn is over and they have to pay a drinking fine. If a player has still not succeeded after three attempts then they are disqualified.

Once everyone has had their turn, an inch is cut from the top of the box, and the next round begins. The box gets smaller each round until only one player remains — the winner!

UNIQUE

CRAZY
COYOTE

CHAIN
REACTION

FULL FLAVOUR

TRADE
MARK

CHAIN REACTION

PLAYERS NEED TO BE SITTING IN A CIRCLE OR IN A LINE AGAINST THE BAR.

Players place both hands on the table or bar in front of them, crossing each hand with the player either side. Thus each person's left hand should be in front of the person on their left and and each person's right hand should be in front of the person on their right. Try it — it's really quite simple!

Someone starts by slapping one of their hands on the table. This should be followed by the next hand on the table and then the next etc. going round in order. This bit is more difficult then it sounds especially when things inevitably speed up!

The owner of any hand that does not slap when required has to take a drink as does any nervous hand that slaps out of turn.

TRADE MARK

1 9 8 8

CRAZY COYOTE

CHASE THE ACE

PREMIUM GAME

CHASE THE ACE

EQUIPMENT: PACK OF CARDS

Each player is dealt one card, face down on the table. Players take turns to look at their card and decide whether to swap it with the person on their left or keep it.

The loser is whoever is left with the lowest card at the end and they have to pay a drinking forfeit.

If a person elects to swap then they have to keep the card passed to them. If a player holds a king (which is unbeatable) they can refuse to swap.

Aces tend to get passed round the table with alarming speed ending up with the poor dealer, so it is only fair that players should take turns at dealing.

CLAPPING

GAME

CLAPPING GAME MADE TO THE HIGHEST STANDARDS. UNSPOILT BY THE DECADES OF PROGRESS. A PREMIUM GAME

CLAPPING GAME

Players sit round a table with their hands flat on the tabletop. The person who starts decides the direction of play and slaps their hands down on the table, one at a time.

The next player follows immediately and play continues round the table. The following variations can be introduced at any time:

- a double slap changes direction of play
- a triple slap means slap alternate hands only
- a quadruple slap means everyone has to take a drink.

Inevitably, the speed of play increases.

Any hesitation or mistakes incur forfeits!

CRAZY COYOTE

OUR FOUNDER COMMANDER WILBURN

COMMANDER

To be played at room temperature

SINCE 1988

COMMANDER

Simon says... for grown-ups! A player is selected to be the commander. Every time they give a command preceded by the word 'Commander', the other players must perform it. If they give the command without the prefix 'Commander', then the players should not perform the deed and indeed anyone doing so must perform a forfeit. Specific commands which should be introduced are:

'Bilibobs' — wave the fingers of both hands up and down quickly.

'High' — hands raised up. Thus 'Bilibobs High' would be raise hands up AND wave fingers.

"Very high" — stand and put hands in the air. "Even higher" — stand on chair with hands raised.

These should be interspersed with 'Low', 'Very low' etc. Commands should be given at a rapid pace just to thoroughly confuse players!

estd 1988

DIRECTIONS

 THE FINGER POINTING IS A
REGISTERED TRADEMARK
OF THE DIRECTIONS BREWING CO.

PREMIUM GAME
CRAZY COYOTE GAMES

LONDON ENGLAND

DIRECTIONS

Player one starts by determining the direction of play. If they place their right hand on the left part of the chest then play goes left, if they place the left hand on the right part of the chest then play goes right. The next player takes up the challenge and can go in either go in the same direction or change direction.

Sounds simple? As the game progresses, however, concentration is definitely called for.

The fifth person must determine the direction by placing both hands on top of each other, and it is the fingers of the top hand which determine the direction. If they point right play goes right; if left, then play goes left.

An additional rule applies to the tenth player who simply points at any other player and the game starts again from that new point.

As usual, hesitations and errors attract drinking fines.

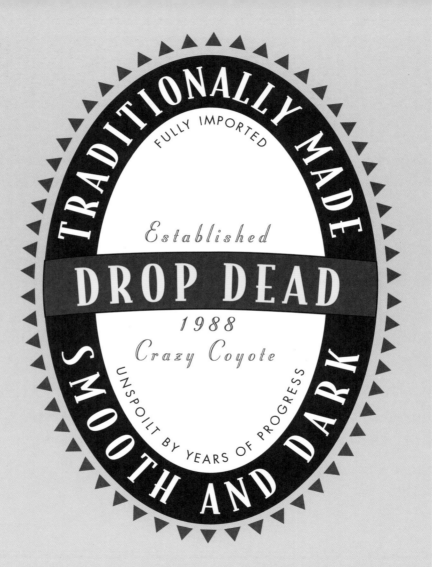

DROP DEAD

EQUIPMENT: FIVE DICE
OBJECTIVE: TO TRY AND SURVIVE LONGEST
AND ACHIEVE THE HIGHEST SCORE!

Players take turns throwing the five dice, trying to get the highest score possible. If anything other than a 2 or 5 is thrown, the total spot value thrown is scored, the player takes a drink and throws again with all five dice.

If a 2 and/or 5 is thrown, the player scores nothing for that throw and any dice which showed 2 or 5 are excluded from their next throw. This time, all the players watching take a drink!

Play continues until the player's last die shows a 2 or 5. They are then said to have 'dropped dead' and this point should be reinforced by a rousing chorus from the other players. Everyone takes a drink.

The score is totaled and play passes to the next person. The winner is the player with the highest score at the end.

Crazy   Coyote

Fingers
& toes

PLAY AT ROOM
TEMPERATURE
-1988-

FINGERS AND TOES

EQUIPMENT: TWO MATCHBOXES

AIM: TO FLICK YOUR MATCHBOX
INTO YOUR PARTNER'S GLASS

Two players sit on chairs opposite each other. Each has a glass on their chair resting between their thighs. The players get a matchbox and, using their forefingers as pivots, rest the box between their thumbs. They must now take turns to flick the box into other's glass.

Each time you succeed, your opponent has to drink two fingers, but scores are cumulative so that if your opponent answers by flicking their matchbox into your glass, you now have to drink four fingers. The forfeit is actually only paid when someone misses, so tension mounts as the game proceeds.

- FIZZ · BUZZ -

AN ADULT

FINE

ESTD
1988

Crazy Coyote

GAMES

DRINKING GAME

FIZZ BUZZ

A QUICK-FIRE COUNTING GAME!

No drinking game compendium would be complete without this gem. Players sit in a circle and play goes round clockwise with players calling out "1", "2", "3" in order. When the number 5 is reached, or any multiple of 5, or indeed any number containing the digit 5, the player must say, "Buzz" instead. Counting then continues round the circle. Once players are adept at this a new rule should be introduced: the digit 7 or any multiple of 7 must be replaced by the word "Fizz". Thus play would go "3, 4, Buzz, 6, Fizz". It gets increasingly more difficult! Should you reach the dizzying heights of 57, this of course would be "Buzz, Fizz".

Anyone who gets it wrong is out — and has to take a drink. Undue hesitation should likewise be punished. The winner is the last remaining player who is declared to be a mathematical genius.

CRAZY COYOTE

4
JACKS

1988

LONDON

4 JACKS

EQUIPMENT: A PACK OF CARDS

This is is a simple warm-up game. A pack of cards is shuffled and the dealer deals out the cards, one to each player, in full view of everyone.

The player who is dealt the first jack has to nominate a long drink. The player who receives the second jack names the chaser. The third jack means the player has to pay for the drinks.

Whoever receives the fourth jack has to drink them!

ADULT DRINKING GAMES

FROGS

PREMIUM

 CRAZY COYOTE

FROGS

Player one starts by saying "One frog, four eyes, four legs, plops into the pond". The second player takes up the challenge by saying "Two frogs, four eyes, eight legs, plop, plop into the pond".

Play continues around the table, adding a plop for each frog.

Undue hesitation will be fined, as, of course, any mathematical errors or mutant frogs.

This is not as easy as it sounds — particularly if played in the late evening!

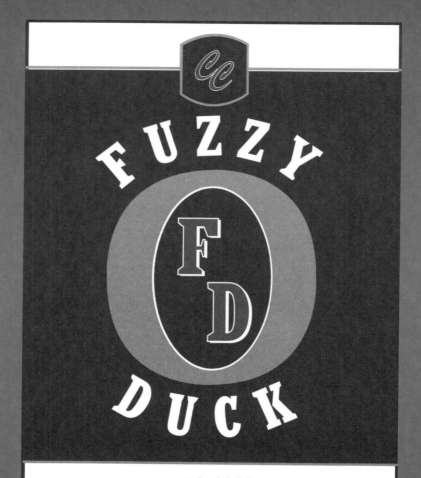

FUZZY DUCK

A TONGUE-TWISTING, CONCENTRATION GAME!

One player starts by saying "Fuzzy Duck" and play passes to their left. The next player can either say "Fuzzy Duck" (in which case play passes to their left) or "Does he?" in which case a) play reverses direction and b) the player on the right says "Ducky Fuzz".

Whenever play is moving in a clockwise direction, players should say "Fuzzy Duck", and when play moves in an counter-clockwise direction say "Ducky Fuzz". Any player can reverse direction with "Does he?" at any time.

Any player speaking out of turn, or saying the wrong thing, pays a minor drinking forfeit. Any player asking a grossly indecent question (play it, if you don't know what we mean!) has to pay a major drinking forfeit or chose a forfeit card.

Giraffe

ADULT DRINKING GAMES

TRADE MARK

SERVE IN A TALL GLASS

Crazy Coyote

GIRAFFE

EQUIPMENT: AN EMPTY MATCHBOX

An empty matchbox cover is placed on the floor. Players take it in turns to kneel down on their hands and knees and try and pick up the box with their nose.

Anyone who falls flat on their face has to drink three fingers and try again. If they fail on their second attempt they are out of the game. In following rounds, the box is moved further away from the kneeling player.

The winner is whoever succeeds in lifting the box from the furthest distance using their nose.

TM

TRADE MARK

HARRY

MANUFACTURED IN THE
UNITED KINGDOM
BY CRAZY COYOTE
GAMES

HARRY

Player one looks at another player and says "Harry?" That player must respond by saying "Yes, Harry?" to which the first player responds by concluding "Tell Harry".

Now it is the other player's turn to say to a third player "Harry?" who should respond by saying "Yes, Harry?" back to the second player who does the same back to the first player to which the first player responds by concluding "Tell Harry". The game moves round the circle, with the question "Yes, Harry?" always being passed back to the first player.

If a player makes a mistake then they become "Harry one spot". It gets increasingly difficult as the game speeds up. An alternative version is to play with the name Bruce for each boy playing and Sheila for each girl. Antipodean accents must be used.

ONLY THE FINEST INGREDIENTS ARE USED IN OUR MAUNUFACTURE

PRODUCED IN THE UNITED KINGDOM BY CRAZY COYOTE GAMES

HI HO

Everyone should know the words to the tune: "Hi Ho, Hi Ho, it's off to work we go, with a shovel and pick and a walking stick, Hi Ho, Hi Ho, Hi Ho, Hi Ho, Hi Ho, it's off to work..."

The players sit round a table, each holding a bottle or can in each hand. They start singing and each time they have sung two words they pass the bottles to the person on their right, and so on.

When the players get to the line which goes "with a shovel and pick", instead of pasing the bottles on, everyone move the bottles to the right and then back again. This happens after every two words, so a total of five times. After 'walking stick', everyone releases the bottles to the person on their right and the song continues.

Chaos will probably ensue, depending at which point in the evening this game is played. Fines should be awarded liberally.

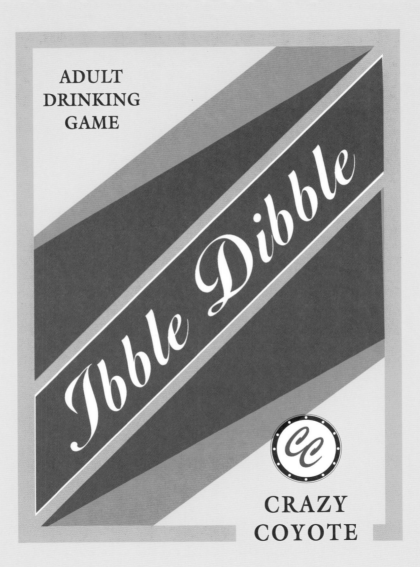

IBBLE DIBBLE

EQUIPMENT: A CORK BLACKENED IN A FLAME OR A PEN.

Players are numbered Ibble Dibble 1, Ibble Dibble 2, etc. going round the table. No.1 starts the game by passing the 'go' to any other player; they could say "Ibble Dibble 1 with no Dobbles , to Ibble Dibble 6 (for example) with no Dobbles" and point to number 6. Number 6 then continues by passing the go to another Ibble Dibble, and so on. This would be easy except for Dobbles.

If a player makes a mistake and says something nonsensical, the cork or pen is used to make a mark (a 'Dobble') on their face. If this happens to player number 4 for instance, they become Ibble Dibble 4 with 1 Dobble, and so on.

If a player points at the wrong player, becomes tongue-tied, or uses the wrong number of Dobbles, they must pay a drinking forfeit.

Made by Crazy Coyote

IN ORDER

Drinking Game
10% alc.

**IN ORDER
OUT OF
ORDER**

IN ORDER

This is an ongoing game which anyone can start up at any point in the evening. It is best to try and catch people unawares!

When there is a lull in proceedings, a player may stand up and say "one". This means the game has commenced!

Someone else must then stand and say "two", followed by another player who says "three" etc.

The only rule is that no two people should stand at the same time (this incurs a three-finger fine for both), and the last person to stand has to down their drink in one!

CRAZY COYOTE

ADULT

THE JUG GAME

ESTD 1988

DRINKING

GAMES

THE JUG GAME

A large jug of beer is needed for this game. The jug is passed around the table and each player drinks as much or as little as they wish.

Tactics come into play as the jug is nearly empty.

The rule is that the person who takes the penultimate drink has to buy the next jug.

Thus there comes a point when each person has to decide whether they can finish what is left in the jug or whether they can risk leaving some, in which case if the next person empties it, the next jug is on you!

ADULT DRINKING GAME

FINE INGREDIENTS AND A LOT OF HARD WORK

TRADE   MARK

· KILLER DARTS ·

GAME · JEU · GIUOCO

PRODUCED IN THE UK

CRAZY COYOTE GAMES OF LONDON

KILLER DARTS

EQUIPMENT: A DARTS BOARD

Players take it in turns to throw a dart with their non-writing hand to determine their number. Any player missing the board at this early stage should be severely penalised.

The aim is to try and become a killer by throwing your number five times. Doubles and triples count as two and three throws.

Once you have become a killer you can try and hit other people's numbers and try to knock down their score. Every time you decrease someone's score by one, they have to pay a drinking fine. If someone is knocked down to minus one, they are out of the game. If you hit your own number while you are a killer then you lose one also — and have to throw your number again before you can regain killer status.

KNEE TREMBLER

Place a large filled glass on the floor about ten feet away. Players take it in turns to drop five coins into the glass, all in one go.

The catch is that the coins must be held between your thighs. Players must still be able to walk and aim at the target.

The result is a variety of very strange and amusing contortions! All the coins must go in in one go; if any escape then that go is invalid.

The last player to succeed has to drink what is in the glass.

Crazy Coyote

Liar Dice

EXPORT

MANUFACTURED IN THE U.K. BY
CRAZY COYOTE GAMES
PURVEYORS OF FINE ADULT DRINKING GAMES

LIAR DICE

EQUIPMENT: FIVE DICE

The first player rolls all five dice, making sure that the others cannot see what he has thrown. He then declares what is being passed to the next player — this may or may not be the truth! The next player can either challenge this or accept. If he accepts, the second player then has to throw any number of the five dice again, telling the others how many he has thrown. He then declares what he is passing on: his score must be higher than the one he received.

SCORING: in descending order of importance
Five of a kind,
Four of a kind,
Full house (three of a kind and two of another),
Three of a kind,
Two pairs,
a pair.

Higher numbers beat lower numbers, so three fives beat three ones. When a player challenges a throw, all five dice are revealed and the loser of the challenge has to pay a drinking forfeit before restarting the game with all five dice.

STRONG

Matchbox
Game

PREMIUM

GOLD
MEDAL

PARIS
1932

Crazy Coyote, London

MATCHBOX GAME

EQUIPMENT: A MATCHBOX

Players sit round a table, each with a drink. Everyone must take it in turns to throw a matchbox over their drink and on to the table. If the matchbox lands on its side, then a two-finger fine is awarded to the next player; if on its end, a four-finger fine is awarded to the next player, and if it lands flat nothing is passed on. The next player then throws and either passes on a new fine or, if the box lies flat, then they have to pay the fine passed on to them. Thus fines are accumulated and only when a player scores nothing does he have to drink.

If the matchbox lands in a drink then the thrower has to drink that drink and, if it belonged to someone else, buy them another one. Players missing the table completely are very sad people and should be dealt with gently but firmly.

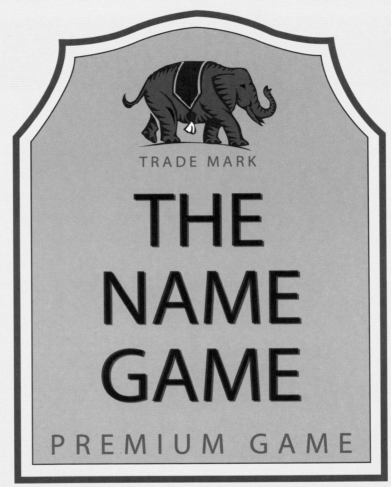

TRADE MARK

THE
NAME
GAME

PREMIUM GAME

CRAZY COYOTE. MANUFACTURERS OF
FINE GAMES FOR QUITE A LONG TIME

THE NAME GAME

A NAME GAME REQUIRING A RAPID RESPONSE!

Players sit in a circle and someone starts by asking a question to which everyone must respond in turn. Each player must respond with a two-word answer, which begins with the initials of their name. Thus if the question is 'What is your favorite food?', Belinda Snodgrass might reply "boiled sweets" and Monty Cartwright might say "melted cheese".

A strict five-second rule must be applied. Players failing to give an answer within the time limit or giving an answer deemed by the group to be substandard, should pay a minor drinking forfeit.

CRAZY COYOTE

FINEST GAMES

OBSTACLE RACE

CRAZY COYOTE GAMES
Hugh Jones
LONDON

OBSTACLE RACE

EQUIPMENT: A DIE

The obstacles consisting of four drinks, preferably all different, are lined up in a row.

The first player starts by rolling the die. They must then decide whether their next throw will be higher or lower. If they guess correctly they can then move past the first drink. The sequence must go alternately higher, lower, higher lower — so if they originally threw higher they cannot move past the second glass until they throw a lower number. Every time they fail they must drink three fingers from the glass proving to be the obstacle.

Once a player has negotiated all the obstacles the glasses are replenished and the second player takes up the challenge.

5·6%

ODDS-ON
FAVORITE

IMPORTED BY THE CRAZY COYOTE CORPORATION
IMPORTERS OF DRINKING GAMES FROM
THE COLONIES AND BEYOND
SINCE 1988

DONCASTER
NEWMARKET
ASCOT
EPSOM
AINTREE

ODDS-ON FAVORITE

EQUIPMENT: A PACK OF CARDS

Each player is dealt a card which they immediately place on their forehead without looking at it.

Players now take turns to bet on whether their card is the highest one. (If a player can see the other cards are an ace, a two and a three they would be tempted to bid quite high — say four fingers).

The cards are revealed and the losers have to drink whatever the winner bid (in this case four fingers) plus their own individual bids.

Beware — reckless bidding will result in a lot of drinking!

PIED PIPER

Each player needs a 'rat'! This is a bottle top with a hole punched through it and a piece of string threaded through and knotted. Players place their rats in a pile in the centre of the table but keep hold of their tails.

A 'rat catcher' is appointed and holds a bowl or large cup downwards at the edge of the table. He counts down "3, 2, 1, Go!" at which point he tries to catch as many rats as possible in the centre of the table while everyone tries to pull their rat to safety.

Players are penalized:

• if their rat is caught (two-finger drinking fine and disqualification from the game)
• if they snatch their rat away too early (four-finger drinking fine but they stay in the game.

The catcher is fined two fingers if he fails to catch any rats. This game can get rather boisterous!

PUB
GOLF

CRAZY COYOTE GAMES

PREMIUM

PUB GOLF

A SERIOUS DRINKING GAME FOR GOLF FANS!

For this pro-am tournament, players organize themselves into pairs, the professional player is the pint drinker and the amateur can either drink shorts or halves. Teams visit nine bars which represent the nine holes of the course. Each 'hole' is par 3 i.e. each drink should be swallowed in three swigs to be 'on par'.

Scores are combined so that if the pro drinks their pint in 4 swigs (i.e. one over par), the amateur needs to finish theirs in 2 to achieve par for the hole. If the pro player downs their drink in one, there is no need to combine scores, the amateur player need not drink for that hole and the team can simply claim a hole-in-one.

Each trip to the bathroom costs one shot, falling over on the course costs two, 'dropping your clubs' or undue spillage risks disqualification. Rules can be adapted to suit the drinking capacity of the players.

PUCKER AND SUCK

MANUFACTURED WITH IMMENSE PRIDE BY THE CRAZY COYOTE CORPORATION

TRADE MARK

ESTD 1988

PUCKER AND SUCK

EQUIPMENT: A CREDIT CARD

This is a much more interesting variation of that children's game where you have to pass a matchbox between your knees or an orange under your chin.

In this version, players have to pass a credit card around in a ring using only their mouths and the power of suction.

The first person places the card flat against their lips and sucks! The next person places their lips against the other side and they must suck while the first person blows. It's a game to get intimate with!

Fines are imposed if the card is dropped or if anyone cheats by using a different part of their body. The game is improved by playing in mixed company.

ALCOHOL 0%

SERGEANT

TRADE MARK

MAJOR

CRAZY COYOTE GAMES, LONDON

GENERAL

SERGEANT MAJOR GENERAL

OBJECTIVE: TO AVOID THE DUNCE'S CHAIR!

Players are assigned ranks according to their position around the table: the first is a general, the player to their right is a major, the next a sergeant, then 1, 2, 3 etc. The last player is labelled 'Dunce'.

The General starts by standing, saying "General" and then somebody else's rank or number. If they say "General, 4" for example, it is now 4's turn to stand, say their number and pass it on to somebody else.

The only rule is that a person may not send it back to the person who has just passed it on or to the person either side of them. If a player does this, stands at the wrong time or hesitates, they have to pay a drinking forfeit and they become the 'dunce'. They take the dunce's seat and everyone in between has to adjust position accordingly, so acquiring new ranks and numbers.

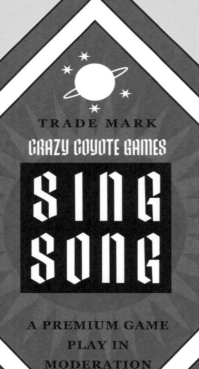

TRADE MARK

CRAZY COYOTE GAMES

SING
SONG

A PREMIUM GAME
PLAY IN
MODERATION

SING SONG

The MC chooses a subject or color: rain, blue, trains etc. Play goes round the table as each player sings a snippet from a song which contains a reference to that object or color.

Thus if 'blue' is chosen, suitable offerings would be: Blue Suede Shoes, Don't It Make Your Brown Eyes Blue, Blue Moon etc.

If a player sings a song already selected, fails to come up with anything or simply sings appallingly then they must pay a hefty drinking fine.

THE LONDON CLASSIC

"DRINKING GAME"

SLAM

CRAZY COYOTE GAMES

estd 1988

another beaut game from ya mates at Crazy Coyote

SLAM

EQUIPMENT: PACK OF PLAYING CARDS

OBJECTIVE: TO GET FOUR OF A KIND AND SLAM!

Prepare the deck of cards using four cards of a kind for each player. Shuffle this thoroughly and place a number of small objects (pennies, matches) in the centre of the table. There should be one less than the number of players. Deal the pack so each player has four mixed cards.

Players examine their cards and, at a given signal, everyone pushes a card they do not want (face down) to the player on their left. Everyone looks at their new card and decides whether to pass it on or exchange it for one from their hand. This continues until someone gets four of a kind. This player should then slam their hand down and quickly grab one of the objects. Everybody else follows suit, leaving someone without an object. This person has to drink a slammer (or other drink) before rejoining the game.

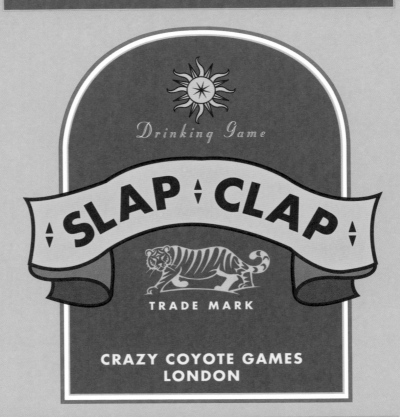

SMOOTH FULL FLAVOR
SERVING INSTRUCTIONS ON REVERSE

Drinking Game

SLAP · CLAP

TRADE MARK

CRAZY COYOTE GAMES
LONDON

PLAY AT ROOM TEMPERATURE

SLAP-CLAP

OBJECTIVE: TO CALL OUT NAMES
WHILE KEEPING IN TIME!

Players sit in a circle and start up a clapping rhythm by:

>   (1) slapping their thighs with both hands, then
>   (2) clapping their hands together and then
>   (3,4) clicking fingers on each hand in turn.

Practice until everyone is keeping the same rhythm!

Player one starts by saying "Names of", (slap, clap) "fam-ous", (click, click) and then he or she must pick a category (beaches, types of car etc.) Each player follows in turn with a suitable word or name. The most important rule is that players can only speak on the finger clicks, so the chosen word must be spread over two syllables to fit the rhythm. ("Bondi-Beach" or "Toy-ota" for example). Anyone who hesitates, breaks the rhythm or who calls out a ridiculously inappropriate word has to take a drink. Categories can be as broad or as limited as you dare.

AN ADULT

SINCE 1988

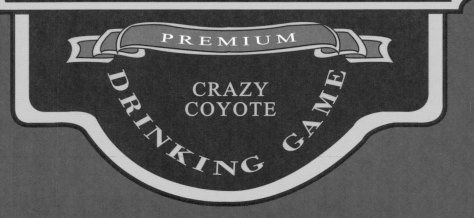

SPOOF

PREMIUM

CRAZY
COYOTE

DRINKING GAME

SPOOF

EQUIPMENT: THREE COINS FOR EACH PLAYER

All players put their hands under the table and place 3, 2, 1, or indeed none of the coins into one of their hands. This hand is the held closed over the table as players take turns to guess the total number of coins held in all the hands.

Players should take turns in making first guess. Once all guesses have been made, everybody opens their hands and all the coins are counted. The person who has guessed correctly can retire safely to watch the next round. Everybody else has to take a drink.

Whoever is left in at the end is the loser and has to undertake a major forfeit.

SPOON

ESTABLISHED ✕ 1 9 8 8

THE CROSSED SPOONS ARE
A TRADEMARK OF CRAZY COYOTE GAMES

GAME

SPOON GAME MANUFACTURERS SINCE THE DAY BEFORE YESTERDAY

SPOON GAME

Two players are pitted against each other, one of whom should be new to the game.

Players sit opposite each other, each with a tablespoon held between their teeth. Each must in turn, bend forward and allow the other to hit them on the back of the head with the spoon. As the spoon is only held in their mouth, this should not really hurt. Play continues until a player drops out.

The trick is that someone stands behind the victim with a larger spoon or ladle. When the victim bends forward, they are dealt a hefty blow by the ladle-holder. They obviously assume it is the other player and try to get their own back which only leads to further suffering and increased frustration. It is hilarious for all onlookers but ultimately you will have to put the victim out of their misery!

STICKY TOFFEE

ESTABLISHED

SINCE 1988

CRAZY COYOTE
LONDON

PUDDING

STICKY TOFFEE PUDDING

OBJECTIVE: TO KEEP YOUR TEETH HIDDEN!

Before the game starts cards should be made with the name of a pudding on each one. Each player is dealt a pudding card and tells the others what their elected pudding is. Players should attempt to memorize these. The first player calls out their pudding name followed by another player's. That player must call out their pudding name followed by another's and so on. The only snag is, that players must talk without showing their teeth.

Any glimpse of tooth enamel, no matter how fleeting, is punished with a drinking forfeit. Laughing is, of course, the most grievous of misdemeanours and should gigglers fail to cover their mouths in time, they should be penalized with a major drinking forfeit. Similarly, players must take care that their speech is intelligible as incoherent speech also attracts a forfeit.

TARGET PRACTICE

EQUIPMENT: A FULL CAN OF SOMETHING FIZZY FOR EACH PLAYER

One of the cans is given a vigorous shaking so that the contents will be well and truly lively!

The cans are then mixed and swapped about so that the shaken can is lost among the others. Alternatively, they could be placed in a bag.

One by one, players select a can and open it six inches from their face with the opening pointing towards them.

Some lucky soul will have to suffer the humilitation of a can of drink exploding in their face.

CRAZY COYOTE GAMES

THINK
AS YOU
DRINK

PREMIUM

THINK AS YOU DRINK

OBJECTIVE: TO THINK QUICKLY
OF FAMOUS NAMES!

Player one starts by calling out a famous person's name — say "Marc Bolan". Player two must follow by calling out a famous person whose first name starts with the letter of the last person's surname. Thus, "Bill Clinton" could follow, then "Cyril Regis" etc.

Whilst a player is thinking of a name to call out, he must drink his drink. Whilst this is happening, other players are at liberty to call out appropriate names thereby disqualifying them. So if someone calls out "Bill Clinton" while you are still drinking ...and thinking...that is a name you cannot use! Players should endeavor to call out as many names as possible so that the drinker is forced to continue drinking until they come up with something original.

If someone calls out a name where both initials are the same — say Marilyn Monroe — then the order of play is reversed.

The Truth Game

estd 1988
Adult Drinking Game

Crazy Coyote Games

THE TRUTH GAME

This needs to be played amongst close friends and intimates! Player one starts by declaring something he has never done: I have never been to or never done something. This can range from visiting a massage parlor to reading a gossip magazine.

Any player who HAS done this thing has to drink one finger.

Any player who denies the deed but is exposed as lying has to drink two fingers.

Whoever is the last to keep some of their drink is the winner but the MC must exert strict control over this game or it may get violent.

WIBBLY WOBBLY

Obstacles are made up of a line of four drinks, preferably varied. The first player starts by rolling a die. They must then decide whether their next throw will be higher or lower. If they guess correctly, they can then move past the first drink.

The sequence must go alternately higher, lower, higher, lower — so if they originally threw higher, they cannot move on past the second glass until they throw a lower number.

Every time they fail, they must drink three fingers from the glass which is proving to be the obstacle.

Once a player has safely negiotated all obstacles, the glasses are replenished and the second player takes up the challenge.

WARNING

We recommend that you play these games with non-alcoholic beverages. However, please read and follow these important instructions and warnings prior to playing any of the following drinking games. Failure to follow these instructions and warnings may result in serious injury or death.

- These drinking games are for adults aged 21 and over only.
- Do not operate a vehicle if you drink alcohol while playing any of these games.
- No-one who must operate a vehicle within 12 hours of playing these games should play any drinking game with alcohol.
- Use plastic bottles or cups or cans only. No glass should be used while playing any drinking game.
- Stop if you feel dizzy or sick whilst playing.
- Do not drink more alcoholic beverages than the legal limit while playing any drinking game.
- Do not play any drinking games where it is against local rules or laws, such as on university campuses.
- In no case should anyone who has consumed alcoholic beverages while playing a drinking game drive a vehicle until at least 12 hours after playing.
- Consult the label of any medication you are taking for limitations of alcohol intake prior to playing any drinking game.
- Women should not drink alcoholic beverages during pregnancy because of the risk of birth defects.
- Consumption of alcoholic beverages impairs your ability to drive a car or operate machinery and may cause health problems.
- We strongly recommend alternatives to drinking forfeits are used to moderate alcohol intake.